A New True Book

BRIDGES

By Norman and Madelyn Carlisle

*This "true book" was prepared
under the direction of
Illa Podendorf,
formerly with the Laboratory School,
University of Chicago*

 CHILDRENS PRESS, CHICAGO

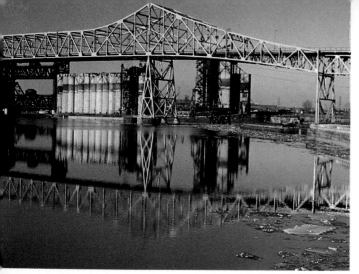

Steel bridge

PHOTO CREDITS

©Ray F. Hillstrom (Hillstrom Stock Photos) — 2, 4, 14, 16 (2 photos), 17 (left), 18, 20 (bottom), 26 (3 photos), 28 (2 photos), 35 (top), 43 (left)

Root Resources — Earl L. Kubis, 37 (bottom)

Bill Thomas — 6

James M. Mejuto — 22, 32, 42 (left)

Al Schaefer — 38

Historical Picture Service, Chicago — 7, 8, 11, 12

Jerome Walczak — 40 (2 photos)

Tony Freeman — 24

Chandler Forman — 9

Italian Government Travel Office — 13

Joseph DiChello, Jr. — 29, 33, 42 (right), 44, 45

Reinhard Brucker — 15, 17 (right)

Julie O'Neil — 43 (right)

James P. Rowan — 19, 35 (bottom)

Jerry Hennen — 20 (top), 39

Hillstrom Stock Photos — ©Howard Levey, 30; ©Norma Morrison, 37 (top); ©Shooter's Photo, Inc., cover

Library of Congress Cataloging in Publication Data

Carlisle, Norman V., 1910-
  Bridges.

  (A New true book)
  Includes index.
  Summary: Briefly discusses the first bridges, famous and unusual bridges, and bridge design and construction.
  1. Bridges — Juvenile literature. [1. Bridges]
I. Carlisle, Madelyn. II. Title.
TG148.C37 1983   624.2   82-17874
ISBN 0-516-01677-6   AACR2

TABLE OF CONTENTS

Log bridge across a river in British Columbia

HOW BRIDGES BEGAN

A long time ago someone found a log and used it. The log was put across a stream. Then the person walked across to the other side.

The first bridge had been built.

Bridges became important.

People could cross a river to better hunting grounds. They could go to trade goods with people who lived on the other side of a river.

Rope bridge with wooden walkway

Drawing made from a sculpture found on ancient
bronze gates shows bridge builders at work.

SOME BRIDGES
OF LONG AGO

All over the world people
built bridges.

They built their bridges
of stone or of wood. But
they built their bridges in
different ways.

Chinese bridge

In China, bridges often
had little eating places on
them. They also had
houses at both ends.
Travelers could rest there
or meet their friends.

Roman arch bridge in Zamora, Spain

Romans built beautiful bridges of stone. They had rounded openings called arches. Some of these old arch bridges are still in use today.

Long ago there was a Persian king named Xerxes (ZERK•seez). He wanted his soldiers to cross a strip of water called the Hellespont. He had them build a bridge that floated.

They put hundreds of small boats side by side. They put a floor on top of the boats.

Drawing of workers building a pontoon bridge hundreds of years ago

Ever since then armies
have used floating bridges.
We call them pontoon
bridges.

Old London Bridge as it looked in 1760. This bridge stood for six hundred years before it was torn down to make way for a new bridge.

Old London Bridge crossed the Thames River in London. It had twenty arches of stone to hold it up. There were many, many buildings on it. Battles were fought on it. People lived on it.

Bridge of Sighs in Venice, Italy

The city of Venice, in Italy, has canals for streets. Bridges cross over the canals. One of the most famous bridges is "The Bridge of Sighs." Once prisoners walked across it from one part of the jail to another.

WHAT KIND OF BRIDGE IS IT?

All bridges do not go over water. Some go over railroad tracks, buildings, or highways.

Bridges that go over land are called viaducts.

Concrete girder bridge

Some bridges are built
on a straight, solid support,
or beam, that reaches from
bank to bank. A bridge
like this is called a girder
bridge.

Girder bridges can be
made of wood. But most
of them are made of
concrete or steel.

Arch bridges have been built since the time of the Romans.

Arches are used in many ways. The roadway can be above the arch. It can be below it. Or it can go right through the middle of it.

Above: This London Bridge was built by Sir John Rennie in 1831. It was taken down and rebuilt in Arizona at Lake Havasu City in 1971.
Right: Steel arch bridge

Truss bridges may have the roadway on top
or between the trusses.

Short pieces of steel put
together in shapes like
these are called trusses.
Trusses make a bridge
stronger. Truss bridges are
often built for trains.

Cantilever bridge

Some bridges have long arms that reach out from a solid base. They are called cantilever bridges.

Suspension means hanging. A suspension bridge hangs from heavy cables. The cables are like

ropes that are made with
many strands of wire.

High towers hold the
cables in place.

Golden Gate
Bridge in San
Francisco is
a suspension
bridge.

Above: The center of this railroad bridge moves up to let the river traffic through.
Right: Bridges over the Chicago River open to let boats through.

BRIDGES THAT MOVE

Some bridges open to let boats go by.

Some come apart in the middle. Each side moves up and back.

There are other bridges that swing.

Some bridges have a center part that can be raised straight up.

George Washington Bridge crosses the Hudson River in New York.

HOW BRIDGES ARE BUILT

Before a bridge can be
built, an engineer must
plan it.

The engineer must think
about many things.

What kind of bridge would be best? How much weight will it have to hold? How hard will the wind push against it? If the bridge is going over water, what kind of supports will be best? How hard will the water push against them?

Engineers plan every part of a bridge. Every

Concrete and steel supports, called piers, hold up this roadway.

single bolt must be shown in drawings that the workmen can follow.

First supports must be built. These are called piers. They are hard to build.

Big machines dig under the water. They dig through mud. They dig through sand. They dig down to solid rock.

Sometimes a huge steel room is built on the river bottom. Its walls come up above the water. It has no roof.

When the walls are in place, all the water is pumped out. Now workers can go into the room.

Many different types of piers can be used to support bridges.

26

The workers clear the bottom of the pier. They pour in a base of concrete. It hardens and sticks tightly to the rock bottom.

Then they build the pier on top of the concrete. They build it in the shape the engineer drew for them. They use concrete with steel inside to make it stronger.

When the piers are ready, the workers build the top of the bridge.

Cranes and boats are used to bring heavy pieces to the bridge.

Sometimes big sections of the bridge are moved into place by boats. They must be moved carefully. Each section has to be put into the exact place where it belongs. This is hard to do.

Close-up of the cables used on the Brooklyn Bridge in New York

For a suspension bridge,
the men build high towers
on top of the piers. Cables
are hung. A walkway for
the workers is built on top

The Brooklyn Bridge is a suspension bridge.

of the cables. It is often made of steel netting.

When a suspension bridge is hung over water, a boat usually takes the first cable across.

Long ago, people wanted to build a bridge near Niagara Falls.

No boat could cross the river, so a boy flew a kite across. A friend on the other side tied the kite string to a tree. Then

Rainbow Bridge
and Tower at
Niagara Falls

heavier cords were pulled across. At last they pulled over a big cable.

Now an arch bridge spans the river.

Workers put thousands of wires together to make one giant cable.

Walkway on a
suspension bridge

It looks like a big pipe when it is finished.

Finally the floor of the bridge is built. It is held up by smaller cables that hang from the big ones.

It takes years to build a big bridge.

SOME UNUSUAL BRIDGES OF THE WORLD

Here are some of the most unusual bridges in the world.

Covered bridges are found all over New England.

Mackinac Bridge in northern Michigan is five miles long.

Covered bridge

Mackinac Bridge

The Kintai (KIN•tye)
Bridge in Japan was
built in 1673. It has five
wooden arch spans and is
the only one of its kind in
the world.

The bridge over Sydney
Harbor in Australia is a
steel arch bridge. It is
1,650 feet long. It was
opened in 1932.

Kintai Bridge is also called the Bridge of the Brocade Sash.

Sydney Harbor Bridge

Queen Emma Pontoon Bridge

The famous "Queen Emma" Pontoon Bridge at Curacao (koo•rah•SOW•oh), Netherlands Antilles, opens to let ships pass into the inner harbor.

Royal Gorge suspension bridge

Royal Gorge Bridge is
the world's highest bridge.
It is more than 1,000 feet
above the Arkansas River
in Colorado.

Right: Verrazano-Narrows
Bridge
Below: Tower Bridge

Boats from all over the world pass under the Verrazano-Narrows Bridge. It crosses the narrows at the entrance to New York Harbor.

Like a gate to the city, the Tower Bridge in London opens to let ships go up the Thames River to dock.

SOMETHING TO THINK ABOUT

Old London Bridge was once the only bridge across the Thames in London. Now there are many.

Manhattan Island is laced by bridges to other parts of New York City and New Jersey.

In many cities, such as Chicago (left) and Paris (above), bridges connect one part of the city to the other part.

Paris began on an island in the Seine. Now people live on both banks of the river. Paris is a city of bridges.

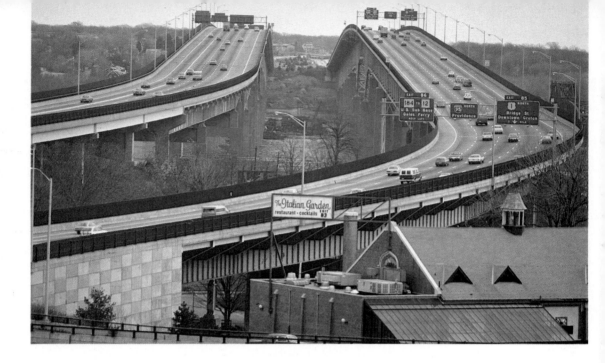

Bridges are many things.

They are beautiful.

They are hard to build.

Cars, trucks, and trains use bridges to go from place to place.

Bridges are important to our world.

Whitestone suspension bridge

45

WORDS YOU SHOULD KNOW

beam(BEEM)—a long, strong piece of wood or metal.
cable(KAY • bil)—a thick, strong rope made of wire.
cantilever(CAN • tih • lee • ver)—a structure that extends
        outward from a support.
engineer(en • jih • NEER)—a person who is trained to plan and
        build structures.
laced(LAYCED)—joined.
pontoon(pon • TOON)—a floating structure.
span(SPAN)—go across.
suspension(sus • PEN • shun)—hanging.
trade(TRAYD)—the business of buying and selling.
truss(TRUHSS)—a frame made in the shape of a triangle.
viaduct(VYE • ah • dukt)—a bridge that goes over land.

INDEX

About the Authors

Writing as a team, Norman and Madelyn Carlisle have published many books for young readers. Their work has appeared in a wide variety of publications, including magazines and newspapers. In addition to raising a family, the Carlisles have traveled extensively in North America and Europe.